Special Symbols:

This workbook is organized to help guide the individual through the training. In addition to the Notes section there are a number of symbols used to help the participant throughout the presentation and workshop. For your convenience these symbols are repeated at the introduction of each section of this workbook.

Suggestion:

This symbol represents a general suggestion relating to your involvement in the presentation and workshop.

Tip:

This symbol represents a tip to the participant which is specific to the subject being taught.

Question:

This symbol represents a question that may be directed to the participant, or meant for the participant to reflect on during the presentation and workshop.

Gem:

This symbol represents bits of Quick and Easy Kaizen wisdom from Norman Bodek himself; use them to ensure successful implementation of your Quick and Easy Kaizen Program.

Table of Contents:

Introduction

Section 1

Section 2

Section 3

Section 4

Quick and Easy Kaizen:
Unlocking Human Potential

Introduction
History of Lean and Quick and Easy Kaizen

Best Viewed at 1024 X 768

Publisher:
Enna Inc.
www.enna.com

Authors
Norman Bodek
Collin McLoughlin

Participant Workbook

Introduction

- The schedule for the training session
- Goals and objectives for Quick and Easy Kaizen
- The history of Lean and Quick and Easy Kaizen

Participant Workbook Provided To:

_____

Suggestion   Tip   Question   Gem

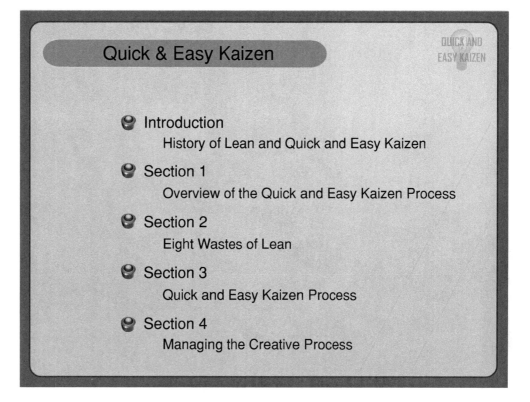

Notes, Slide 2:

_____

_____

_____

_____

_____

_____

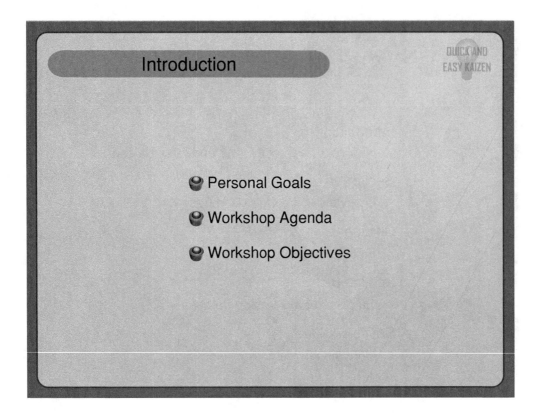

Notes, Slide 3:

_____

_____

_____

_____

_____

_____

_____

Tip:
Write out your personal workshop goal so that you may refer back to it.

_____

History of Quick and Easy Kaizen

- Taiichi Ohno
- Toyota Motor Corporation
- Henry Ford
- Nippon Denso

Notes, Slide 4:

_____

_____

_____

_____

_____

_____

Gem:
People make a difference in the work place.

Question:
Who is considered the Father of Lean manufacturing?

_____

_____

History of Quick and Easy Kaizen

- Taiichi Ohno
- Toyota Motor Corporation
- Henry Ford
- Nippon Denso

Notes, Slide 4, continued:

_____

_____

_____

_____

_____

_____

Tip:
Lean manufacturing is relatively new. It is necessary to adopt Lean manufacturing methods because they are more effective than past methods.

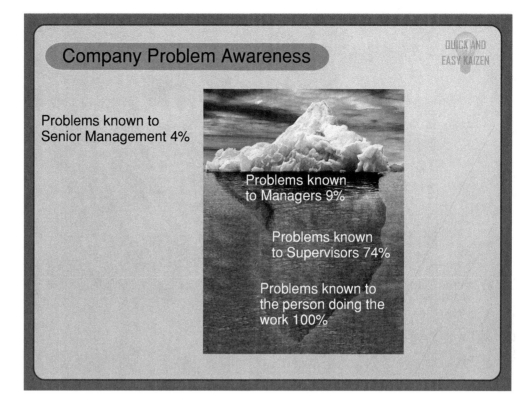

Notes, Slide 5:

_____

_____

_____

_____

_____

_____

Suggestion:
Offer your input throughout the presentation. Each participant is encouraged to contribute to the workshop.

Thinking Production System

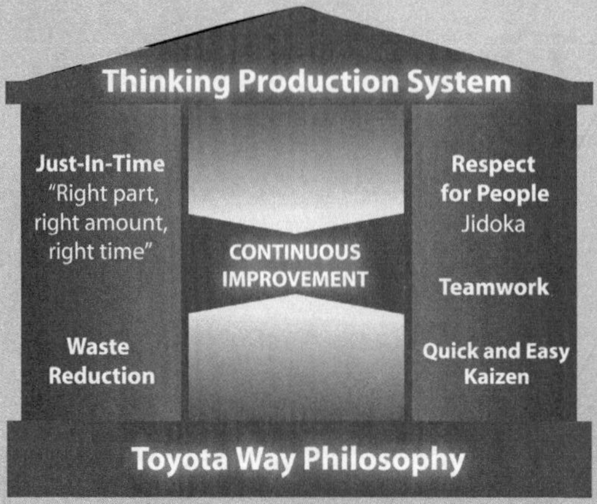

- Jeffrey Liker; The Toyota Way
- Norman Bodek; Thinking Production System
- Toyota House
- Two Pillars

Notes, Slide 6:

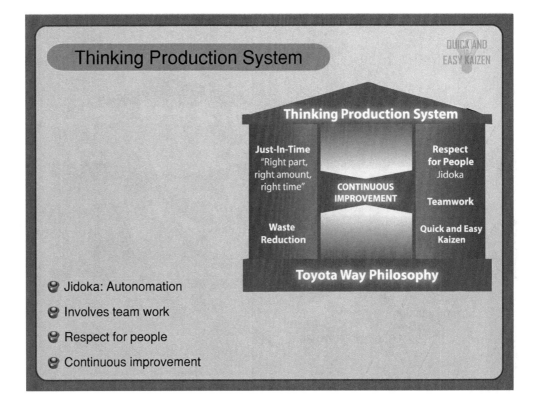

Notes, Slide 7:

_____

_____

_____

_____

_____

_____

Tip:
Traditional understanding of production does not address separating people and machines. In America we focus more on the advancement of electronics and the functionality of machines rather than how effectively people and machines work together.

Thinking Production System

Thinking Production System

Just-In-Time
"Right part, right amount, right time"

Waste Reduction

CONTINUOUS IMPROVEMENT

Respect for People
Jidoka

Teamwork

Quick and Easy Kaizen

Toyota Way Philosophy

- Difference with people focus
- Flow production
- System of continuous improvement

Notes, Slide 8:

_____

_____

_____

_____

_____

_____

Tip:
Ask the Facilitator for some books on Lean. Understanding more about the subject is a great benefit for you personally and professionally.

Gem:
Find new ways to do things quickly, and skip doing unnecessary activities.

Setting Us Apart

Every Toyota team member is empowered with the ability to improve their work environment. This includes everything from quality and safety to the environment and productivity. Improvements and suggestions by team members are the cornerstone of Toyota's success.

- Incredible respect
- 1.5 million ideas per annum
- United States: 1 idea per 7 years implemented

Notes, Slide 9:

_____

_____

_____

_____

_____

_____

_____

Tip:
This workshop is structured in a teach-do format. This means that you will first learn concepts, then apply them in a practical setting.

Question:
What will set us apart from our competition?

_____

_____

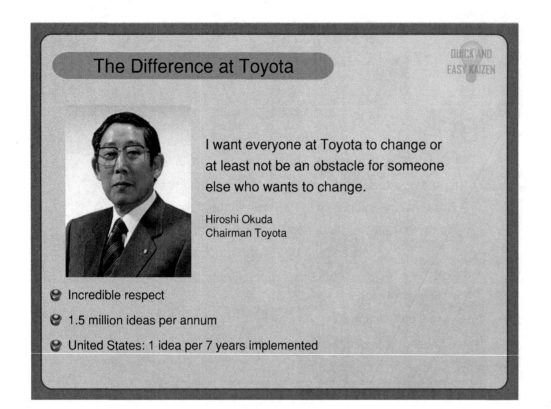

The Difference at Toyota

QUICK AND
EASY KAIZEN

I want everyone at Toyota to change or at least not be an obstacle for someone else who wants to change.

Hiroshi Okuda
Chairman Toyota

- Incredible respect
- 1.5 million ideas per annum
- United States: 1 idea per 7 years implemented

Notes, Slide 10:

_____

_____

_____

_____

_____

_____

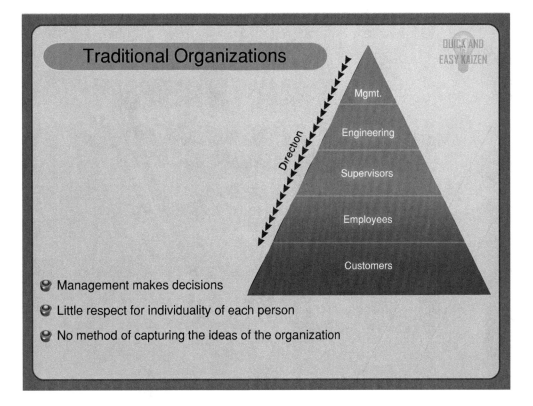

Notes, Slide 11:

_____

_____

_____

_____

_____

_____

Tip:
This pyramid diagram was originally developed to communicate how upper management addressed strategic issues and the lower levels dealt with operational issues. However, in this structure there is a lack of feedback from the workers performing the work.

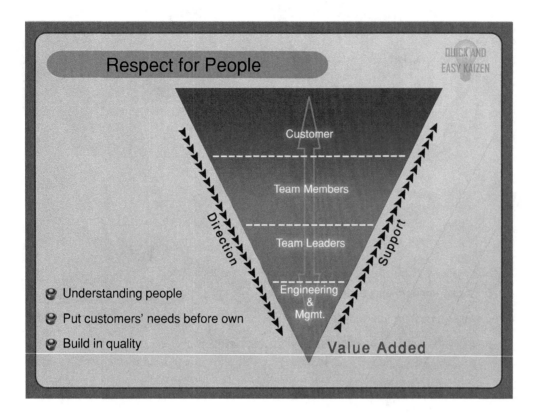

Notes, Slide 12:

_____

_____

_____

_____

_____

Tip:
Understanding the concept of the internal customer is critical to the success of Quick and Easy Kaizen. Ensure that you fully understand this concept; if you do not ask the Facilitator to clarify it for you.

Notes, Slide 13:

_____

_____

_____

_____

_____

_____

Section 1
Overview of the Quick and Easy Kaizen Process

Participant Workbook

Section 1

- Overview of creativity
- Defining Kaizen - Methods, Small ideas, Resistance
- A simple and effective process of change

Suggestion   Tip   Question   Gem

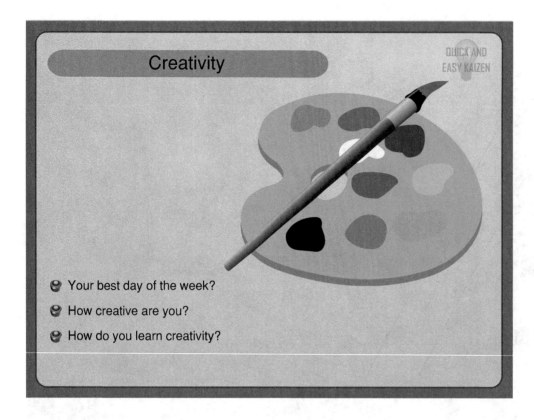

Notes, Slide 15:

_____

_____

_____

_____

_____

_____

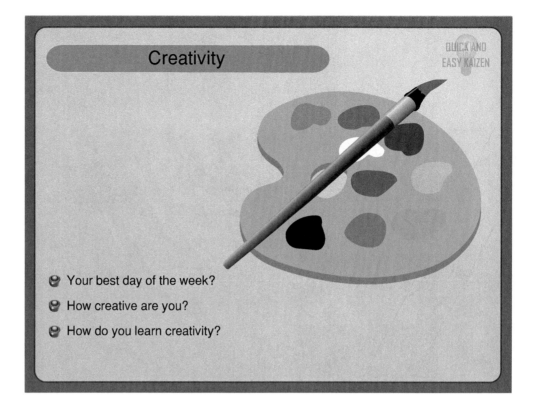

Notes, Slide 15, continued:

_____

_____

_____

_____

_____

_____

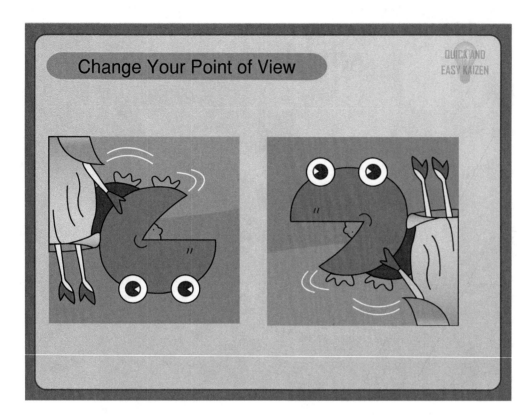

Notes, Slide 16:

_____

_____

_____

_____

_____

_____

Tip:
Offer your own example of something that can be seen from two different perspectives.

Question:
What did you first see when this picture was revealed to you?

_____

_____

Notes, Slide 17:

_____

_____

_____

_____

_____

_____

_____

Suggestion:
Provide feedback when
asked by the
Facilitator.

Question:
Can you provide examples from your work area where there are two
possible viewpoints?

_____

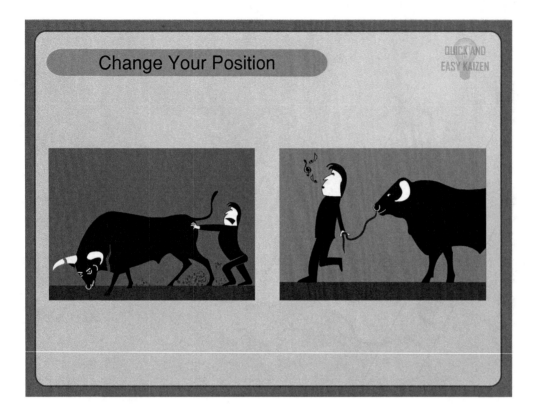

Change Your Position

Notes, Slide 18:

Gem:
Kaizen is changing the method for the purpose of improving. A shortcut in the process without changing the method is negligent.

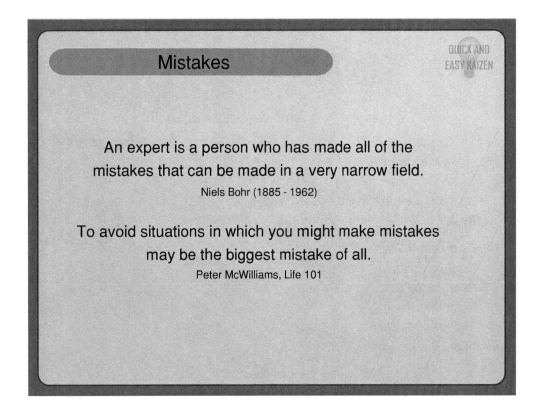

Mistakes

QUICK AND
EASY KAIZEN

An expert is a person who has made all of the
mistakes that can be made in a very narrow field.

Niels Bohr (1885 - 1962)

To avoid situations in which you might make mistakes
may be the biggest mistake of all.

Peter McWilliams, Life 101

Notes, Slide 19:

Suggestion:
Volunteer to read the
quotes aloud.

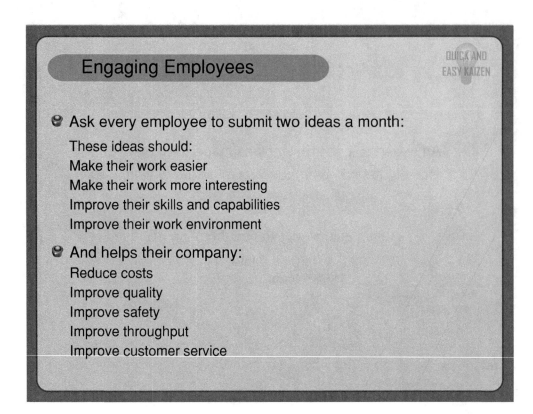

Notes, Slide 20:

_____

_____

_____

_____

_____

_____

Tip:
A business' only way to stay competitive is to constantly reduce the time it takes to manufacture products. If it takes less time to produce we can stay competitive in the industry.

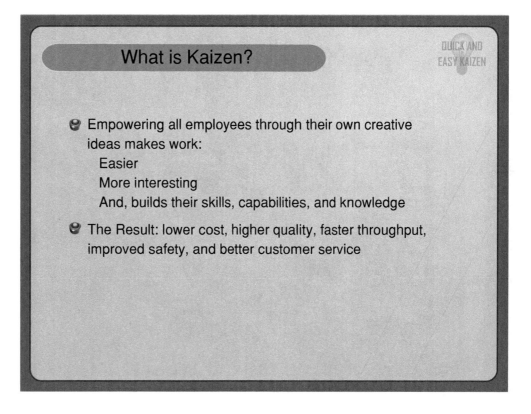

What is Kaizen?

QUICK AND
EASY KAIZEN

- Empowering all employees through their own creative ideas makes work:
  Easier
  More interesting
  And, builds their skills, capabilities, and knowledge

- The Result: lower cost, higher quality, faster throughput, improved safety, and better customer service

Notes, Slide 21:

_____

_____

_____

_____

_____

_____

Gem:
Lean is an accumulation of small changes little by little. Quick and Easy Kaizen focuses on small changes and encourages all employees to be involved in improvement activities.

Notes, Slide 22:

_____

_____

_____

_____

_____

_____

Notes, Slide 22, continued:

_____

_____

_____

_____

_____

_____

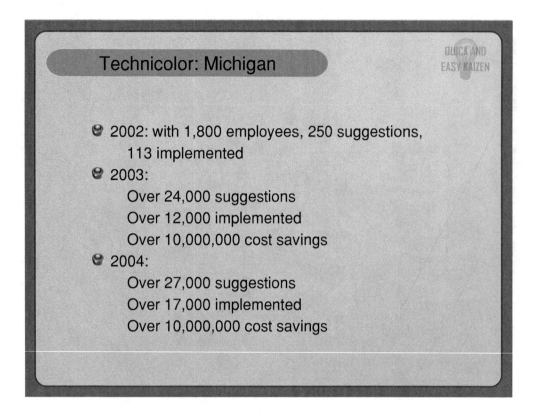

Technicolor: Michigan

QUICK AND EASY KAIZEN

- 2002: with 1,800 employees, 250 suggestions, 113 implemented
- 2003:
  - Over 24,000 suggestions
  - Over 12,000 implemented
  - Over 10,000,000 cost savings
- 2004:
  - Over 27,000 suggestions
  - Over 17,000 implemented
  - Over 10,000,000 cost savings

Notes, Slide 23:

_____

_____

_____

_____

_____

_____

Gem:
Kaizen allows for continuous trial and error.

Notes, Slide 24:

_____

_____

_____

_____

_____

_____

_____

Suggestion:
Refer to the posters as
they summarize key
concepts and ideas.

Notes, Slide 24, continued:

_____

_____

_____

_____

_____

_____

Section 2
Eight Wastes of Lean

Participant Workbook

Section 2

- The Eight Wastes of Lean
- Examples of Quick and Easy Kaizen
- Quick and Easy Kaizen opportunities in our company

Suggestion   Tip   Question   Gem

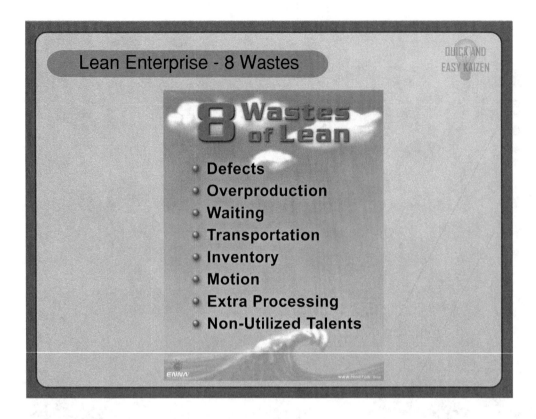

Notes, Slide 26:

<u>Defects:</u> Defects are parts made incorrectly, having excess scrap materials, being provided with the wrong information, and/or having to rework parts.

<u>Overproduction:</u> Overproduction occurs when we produce more than the next process truly needs at the present time.

<u>Waiting:</u> Waiting is time when materials, machines, or information are not ready for us.

<u>Transportation:</u> Transportation, by definition, is moving materials or information from one spot to another spot.

<u>Inventory:</u> Any material that we have other than what is needed immediately is considered waste.

Tip:
Pay particular attention to each definition of the Eight Wastes. These are extremely important as they help you implement Quick and Easy Kaizen.

_____

_____

_____

_____

_____

_____

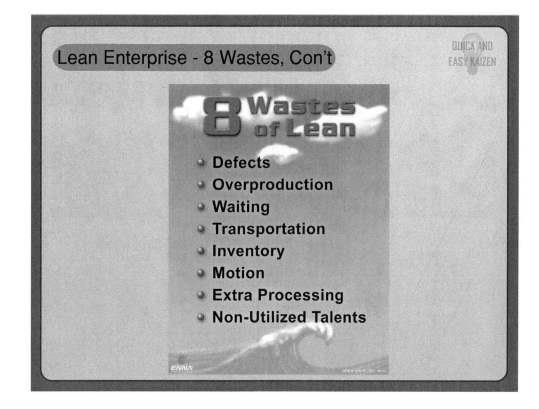

Notes, Slide 27:

<u>Motion:</u> Motion is any movement of people that does not add value to the product or service.

<u>Extra Processing:</u> Extra Processing is activity that adds no value to the product or service from the viewpoint of the customer.

<u>Non-Utilized Talents:</u> Non-Utilized Talents occurs when our minds are not being used to their full potentials to make work easier and more interesting, and eliminating wastes in the process.

Gem:
The Eight Wastes of Lean are at the root of success. Quick and Easy Kaizen aims to eliminate the wastes one at a time.

_____

_____

_____

_____

_____

_____

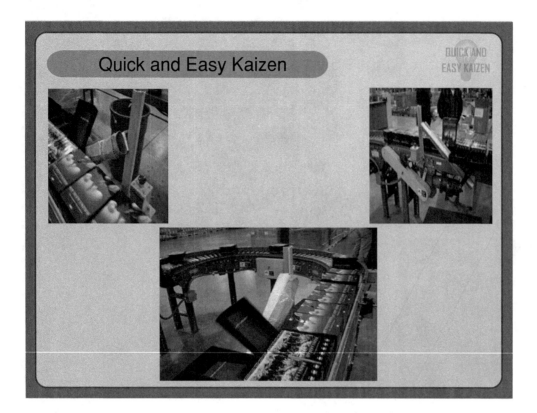

Notes, Slide 28:

_____

_____

_____

_____

_____

_____

Suggestion:
You are encouraged to discuss the different examples and issues with your colleagues.

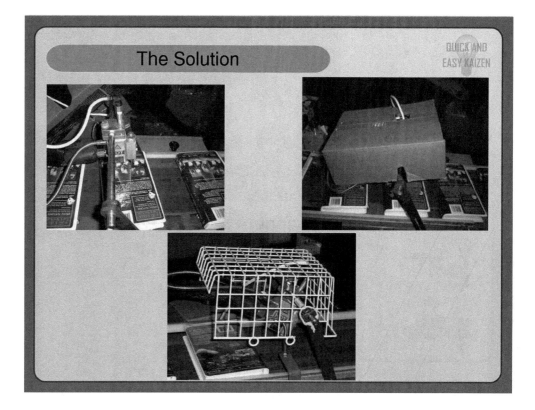

Notes, Slide 29:

_____

_____

_____

_____

_____

_____

3 Rules of Kaizen

Stop - Doing unnecessary things.

Reduce - If you can't stop, try to reduce them somehow.

Change - Try another way.

Notes, Slide 30:

_____

_____

_____

_____

_____

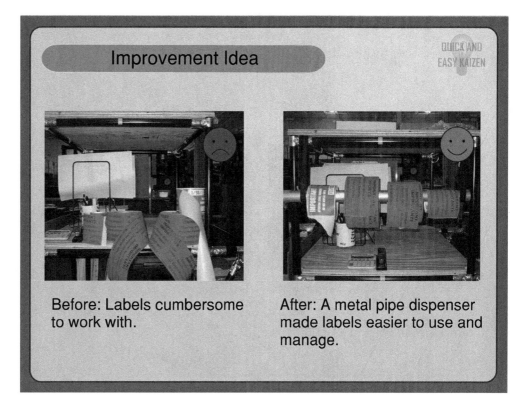

Improvement Idea

Before: Labels cumbersome to work with.

After: A metal pipe dispenser made labels easier to use and manage.

Notes, Slide 31:

_____

_____

_____

_____

_____

_____

_____

Tip:
Provide any ideas you have that are similar to the ones in the illustrations.

Question:
Do you have any examples like this in your area? If so, write them down.

_____

_____

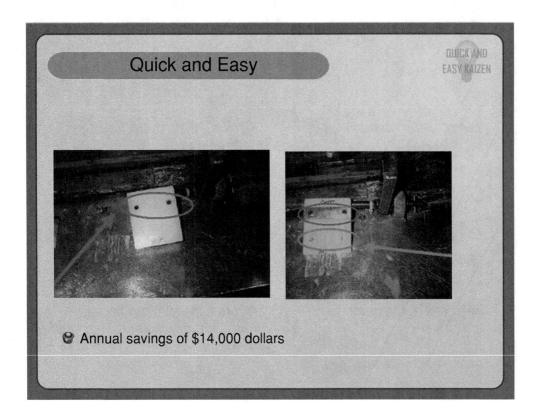

Quick and Easy

Annual savings of $14,000 dollars

Notes, Slide 32:

_____

_____

_____

_____

_____

_____

Tip:
Combine ideas together to reduce or even eliminate time.

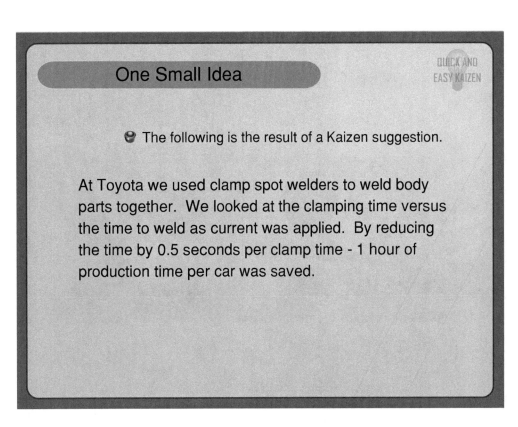

One Small Idea

QUICK AND
EASY KAIZEN

The following is the result of a Kaizen suggestion.

At Toyota we used clamp spot welders to weld body parts together. We looked at the clamping time versus the time to weld as current was applied. By reducing the time by 0.5 seconds per clamp time - 1 hour of production time per car was saved.

Notes, Slide 33:

_____

_____

_____

_____

_____

_____

Gem:
We need to come up with ideas that are within our limited budget. If we only have three people available to do the job, the method used must only require three people. That is Kaizen.

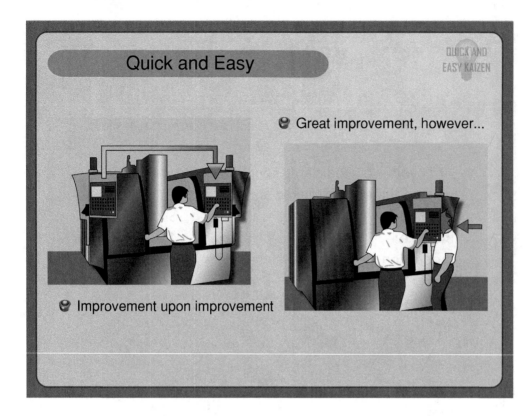

Notes, Slide 34:

_____

_____

_____

_____

_____

_____

Tip:
Even with great ideas safety issues must be considered.

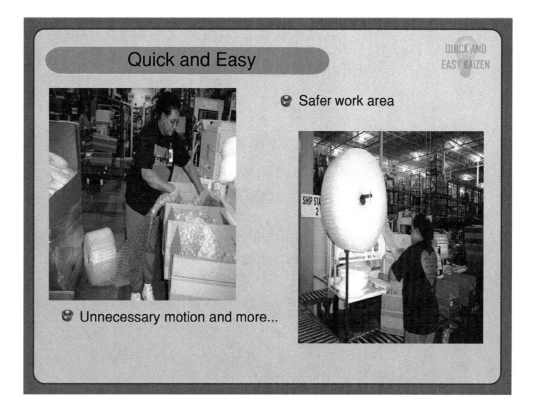

Notes, Slide 35:

_____

_____

_____

_____

_____

_____

Question:
In your own words summarize the solution to the above problem.

_____

_____

3 Reasons for this system

REASONS

- A CONSCIOUS effort
- To have improvement activities CONTINUE
- Improvement becomes an organization-wide effort INVOLVING ALL EMPLOYEES

Notes, Slide 36:

_____

_____

_____

_____

_____

_____

Tip:
Involve many people in the discussions of how Quick and Easy Kaizen will work for your company.

Section 3
Quick and Easy Kaizen Process

Participant Workbook

Section 3

- Define the Quick and Easy Kaizen process
- Write up two problems, two solutions, and their effects
- Share ideas with the group

Suggestion   Tip   Question   Gem

Quick and Easy Kaizen Form

- Date Identified
- Employee Name
- Department
- Idea Number
- Employee Number
- Work Area
- Before Improvement
- Suggested Improvement

Q&E Kaizen Form

Date Identified: _____ Idea No: _____

General Information:

Employee Name: _____ Employee Number: _____

Department: _____ Work Area: _____

Before Improvement:

Suggested Improvement:

Gem:
It is your responsibility to do your job in the best way possible. If you can find a way to do the same job more easily, more comfortably, and with greater quality and productivity, implement the idea.

Tip:
You should have three Quick and Easy Kaizen Forms at this point - one to practice on and two others to document your first Quick and Easy Kaizen Ideas.

Notes, Slide 38:

_____

_____

_____

_____

_____

Quick and Easy Kaizen Form

- Impact Statement
- Verifying Information
- Category
- Eight Wastes
- Office Use Only

Impact Statement:

Verifying Information:

Supervisor: _____

Estimated Cost Saving: _____

Poka-Yoke: ☐ Yes   ☐ No

Pictures: Before ☐ Yes   ☐ No
After ☐ Yes   ☐ No

Category:

☐ Better Process   ☐ Customer Service   ☐ Cost Saving   ☐ High Quality   ☐ Safety

☐ Temporary Fix   ☐ Long Term Fix   ☐ Implemented   ☐ Not Implemented

Eight Wastes:

☐ Movement   ☐ Non-Utilized Talents   ☐ Inventory
☐ Defects   ☐ Overproduction   ☐ Waiting
☐ Process   ☐ Transportation

Office Use Only:

Input Data: ☐ Yes   ☐ No
Import Pictures: Before ☐ Yes   ☐ No
After ☐ Yes   ☐ No

ENNA

www.enna.com

QUICK AND EASY KAIZEN

Notes, Slide 39:

_____

_____

_____

_____

_____

_____

Tip:
As the Facilitator explains this form ask questions to cement your understanding of it.

Quick and Easy Kaizen Process

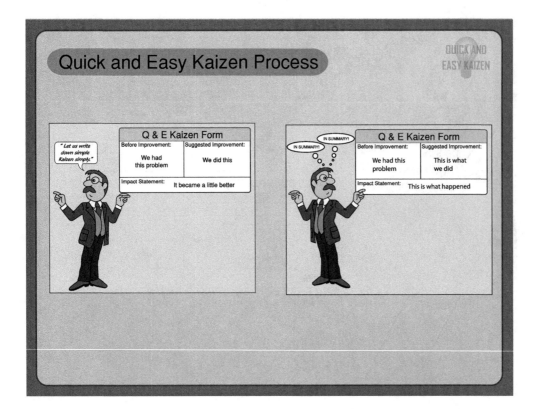

Tip:
Focus on getting your ideas on paper. Do not be concerned about spelling or grammar. Think in summary so that you communicate concisely. Draw a picture if necessary.

Notes, Slide 40:

Tip:
Take time to clarify the concepts with the Facilitator.

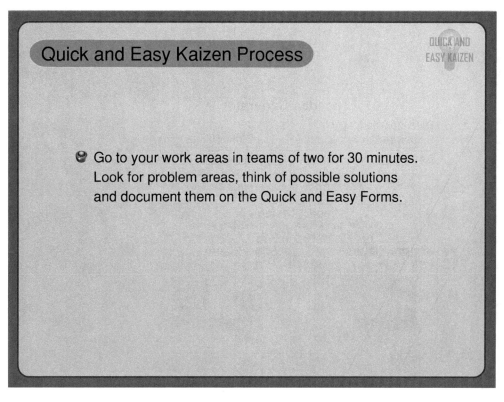

Quick and Easy Kaizen Process

Go to your work areas in teams of two for 30 minutes. Look for problem areas, think of possible solutions and document them on the Quick and Easy Forms.

Notes, Slide 41:

_____

_____

_____

_____

_____

_____

Tip:
Spend as much time as possible in your work area discussing and summarizing your Quick and Easy Kaizen ideas.

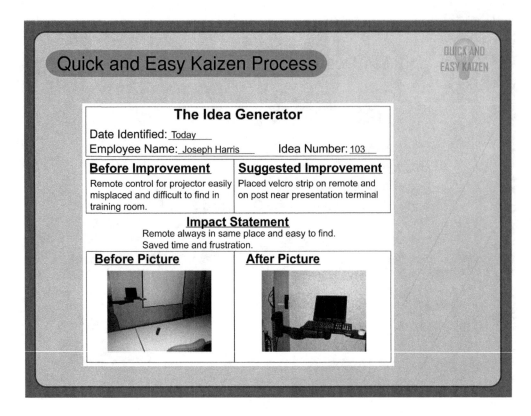

Quick and Easy Kaizen Process

The Idea Generator

Date Identified: Today

Employee Name: Joseph Harris   Idea Number: 103

Before Improvement	Suggested Improvement
Remote control for projector easily misplaced and difficult to find in training room.	Placed velcro strip on remote and on post near presentation terminal

Impact Statement
Remote always in same place and easy to find.
Saved time and frustration.

Before Picture	After Picture

Notes, Slide 42:

_____

_____

_____

_____

_____

_____

Tip:
Expect to share your ideas with the group.

Suggestion:
Take time to help others understand the concepts.

Notes, Slide 43:

_____

_____

_____

_____

_____

_____

Gem:
Quick and Easy Kaizen is a small element to add to your routine. When we all are involved in improvement activities on a regular and continuous basis, it becomes powerful and meaningful to everyone.

Participant Workbook

Section 4

- Formalities of Quick and Easy Kaizen
- Suggested structure and organization of the creative process
- Management and employee responsibilities
- A challenge to create a climate of continuous improvement

Suggestion   Tip   Question   Gem

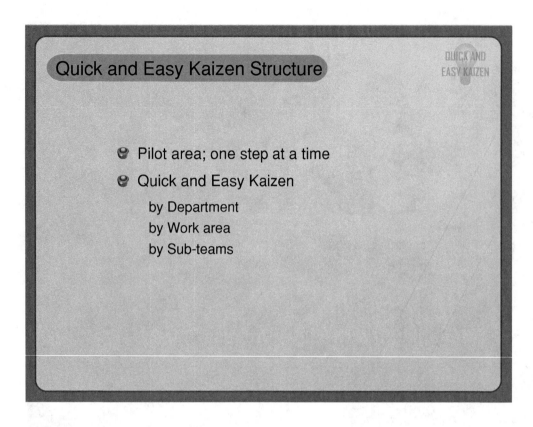

Quick and Easy Kaizen Structure

- Pilot area; one step at a time
- Quick and Easy Kaizen
    by Department
    by Work area
    by Sub-teams

Notes, Slide 45:

_____

_____

_____

_____

_____

_____

Tip:
Look for small ideas that are within your area of responsibility. Work on these issues first instead of ideas that may encompass several departments.

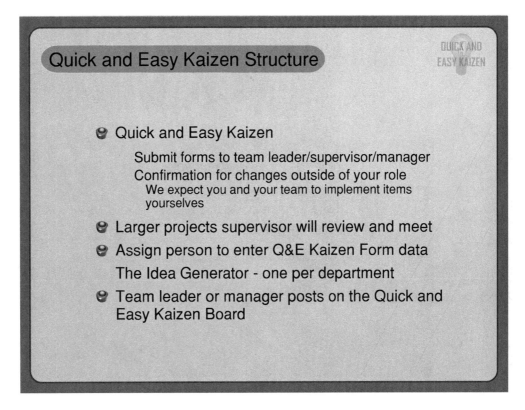

Quick and Easy Kaizen Structure

- Quick and Easy Kaizen
  - Submit forms to team leader/supervisor/manager
  - Confirmation for changes outside of your role
    - We expect you and your team to implement items yourselves
- Larger projects supervisor will review and meet
- Assign person to enter Q&E Kaizen Form data
  - The Idea Generator - one per department
- Team leader or manager posts on the Quick and Easy Kaizen Board

Notes, Slide 46:

_____

_____

_____

_____

_____

_____

Gem:

If we are trying to do the very best from the beginning, often we cannot even get started.

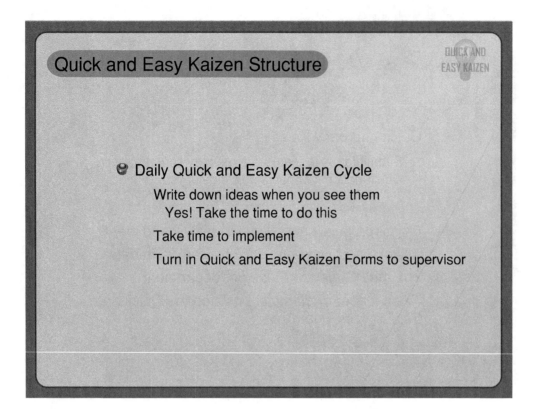

Quick and Easy Kaizen Structure

- Daily Quick and Easy Kaizen Cycle
    - Write down ideas when you see them
        - Yes! Take the time to do this
    - Take time to implement
    - Turn in Quick and Easy Kaizen Forms to supervisor

Notes, Slide 47:

_____

_____

_____

_____

_____

_____

Tip:
All initiatives should be simple and easily implemented by you. However, remember to document each and every idea.

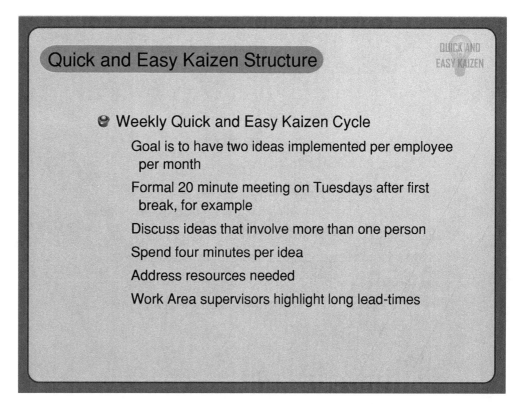

Notes, Slide 48:

_____

_____

_____

_____

_____

_____

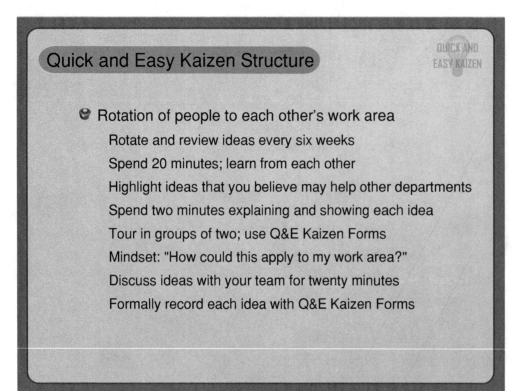

Quick and Easy Kaizen Structure

- Rotation of people to each other's work area
  - Rotate and review ideas every six weeks
  - Spend 20 minutes; learn from each other
  - Highlight ideas that you believe may help other departments
  - Spend two minutes explaining and showing each idea
  - Tour in groups of two; use Q&E Kaizen Forms
  - Mindset: "How could this apply to my work area?"
  - Discuss ideas with your team for twenty minutes
  - Formally record each idea with Q&E Kaizen Forms

Notes, Slide 49:

_____

_____

_____

_____

_____

_____

Tip:
Sharing your ideas with others will unlock the true potential of everyone.

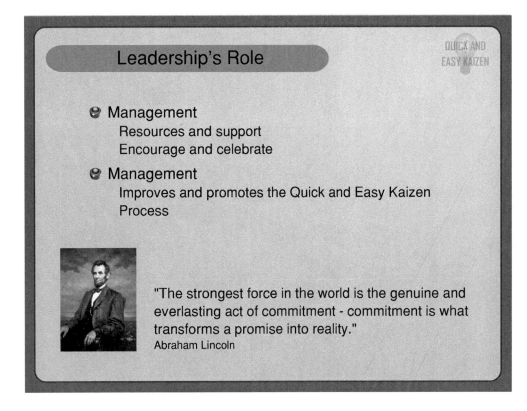

Notes, Slide 50:

_____

_____

_____

_____

_____

_____

Gem:

When people notice problems on their own, they are more inclined to solve them on their own. This is why we emphasize Quick and Easy Kaizen - it comes down to individual participation.

Quick and Easy Kaizen Assessment

Facilitator: _____   Name: _____

Workshop: _____   Date: _____

Circle or write the answer that best fits the question or completes the statement.

1. **Quick and Easy Kaizen originated from __.**
   a) Henry Ford
   b) Jeffrey Liker
   c) Norman Bodek

2. **Of all the problems we have how many are known to upper management?**
   a) 100 percent
   b) 40 percent
   c) 4 percent

3. **Norman Bodek calls the TPS system the __.**
   a) Toyota Production System
   b) Thinking Production System
   c) Total Productive System

4. **What number of ideas per month is our goal?**
   a) Two ideas implemented per employee per month
   b) Two ideas per employee per month
   c) Two ideas implemented per employee per week

5. **Respect for people is the Toyota way because it allows for __.**
   a) management to tell employees what to do
   b) customers' needs first and bi-directional communication
   c) only lateral communication between employees

6. **Quick and Easy Kaizen asks you to __.**
   a) check your brains at the door when you get to work
   b) discuss issues with your supervisor
   c) use your brain every single day

7. **How creative are you, past and present?**
   a) Past, 95% creative; now, 2% of adults are creative
   b) Past, 100% creative; now, I am told 0% creative
   c) Past, 90% creative; now, must only be 10% creative

8. **How do we become an expert?**
   a) By making as many mistakes as possible
   b) Studying a field of knowledge but not practicing
   c) Avoiding situations in which mistakes may be made

9. **Of the 8 Wastes of Lean which one is the worst?**
   a) Transportation
   b) Overproduction
   c) Defects

10. **The Three Rules of Kaizen as explained by Norman Bodek are __.**
    a) slowdown, maximize, and only one way
    b) reconsider, resize, and reuse
    c) stop, reduce, and change

11. **What is the control document of Quick and Easy Kaizen?**
    a) The Conformance Sheet
    b) The Quick and Easy Kaizen Form
    c) The Idea Generator Form

12. **When you write up an idea you need to think in specific terms; one would say to think __.**
    a) in summary
    b) perfect thoughts
    c) randomly, so no one can understand the idea

13. **Writing up an idea should be concise and only take __.**
    a) the time you need to write it down
    b) the same amount of time as the slowest person
    c) two to three minutes maximum

14. **To develop a proper Quick and Easy Kaizen System we need the commitment of __.**
    a) resources, management, employees, and to our customers
    b) employees so that we can do this on our own
    c) resources, management, and employees

1:c, 2:c, 3:b, 4:a, 5:b, 6:c, 7:a, 8:a, 9:b, 10:c, 11:b, 12:a, 13:c, 14:a